Fact Finders®

Awesome ENGINEERING

SKYSCRAPERS

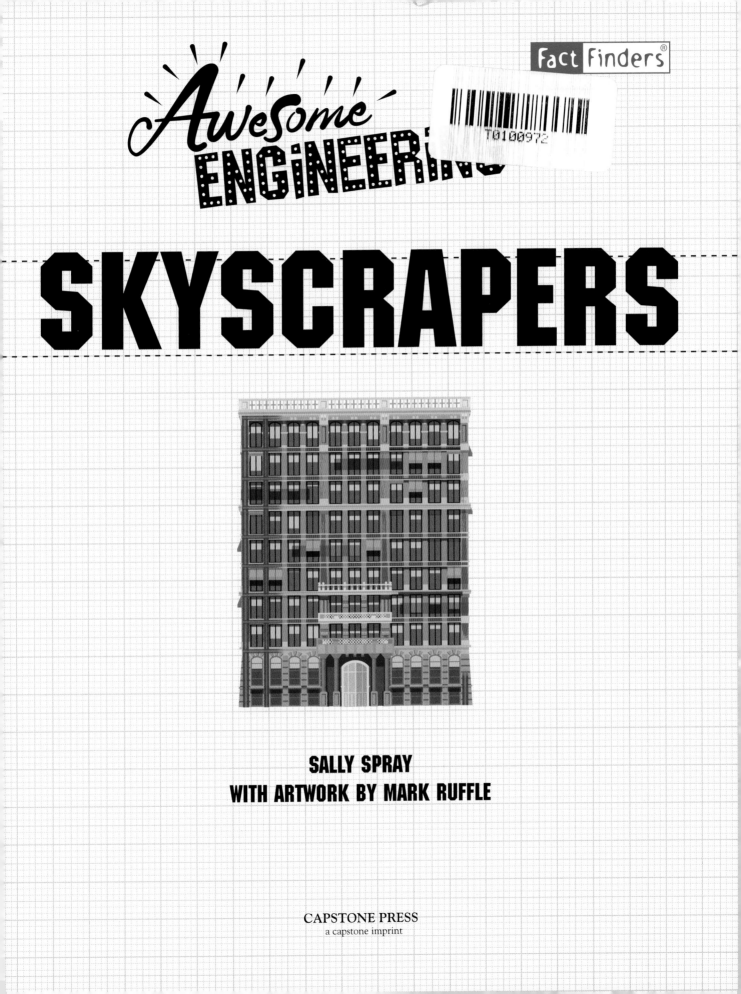

SALLY SPRAY

WITH ARTWORK BY MARK RUFFLE

CAPSTONE PRESS
a capstone imprint

Fact Finders Books are published by Capstone Press,
1710 Roe Crest Drive, North Mankato, Minnesota 56003
www.mycapstone.com

Library of Congress Cataloging-in-Publication Data
Library of Congress Cataloging-in-Publication data is available on the Library of Congress website.

978-1-5435-1333-2 (library binding)
978-1-5435-1339-4 (paperback)

Editorial Credits

Series editor: Paul Rockett
Series design and illustration: Mark Ruffle
www.rufflebrothers.com
Consultant:
Andrew Woodward BEng (Hons) CEng MICE FCIArb

Photo Credits

Aniza/Dreamstime: 28cl. Azat1976/Shutterstock: 23b. Goran Cakmazovic/Shutterstock: 8b. ESB
Professional/Shutterstock: 18t. estherspoon/Shutterstock: 28r. Everett Historical/Shutterstock: 11t.
Julien Hautcoeur/Shutterstock: 13b. Philip Lange/Shutterstock: 20t. Jianhua Liang/Dreamstime:
29tc. Mandritoiu/Dreamstime: 5. Mikhail Markovskiy/Shutterstock: 29tr. Shaiful Zamri Masri/
Dreamstime: 28c. George Rinhart/Corbis Historical/Getty Images: 6. TonyV3112/Shutterstock: 26.
Konstantin Tronin/Shutterstock: 25cr. Thor Jorgen Udvang/Shutterstock: 29tl. Tao Chuen Yeh/AFP/
Getty Images: 18b.

First published in Great Britain in 2017
by The Watts Publishing Group
Copyright © The Watts Publishing Group, 2017

Printed and bound in China.
010755S18

TABLE OF CONTENTS

BUILD IT TALL

Skyscrapers shape our city skylines. They reach jaw-dropping heights and create unusual and wondrous shapes. Building tall and inspiring skyscrapers all over the world requires ambition, imagination, and engineering genius.

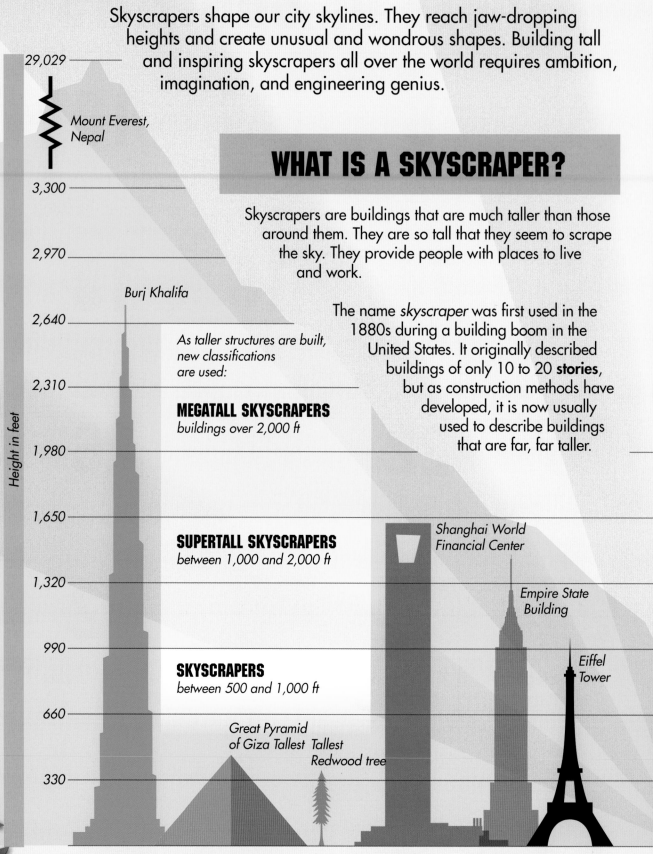

29,029 — Mount Everest, Nepal

3,300 —

2,970 —

Burj Khalifa
2,640 —

2,310 —

1,980 —

1,650 —

1,320 —

990 —

660 —

330 —

Height in feet

WHAT IS A SKYSCRAPER?

Skyscrapers are buildings that are much taller than those around them. They are so tall that they seem to scrape the sky. They provide people with places to live and work.

The name *skyscraper* was first used in the 1880s during a building boom in the United States. It originally described buildings of only 10 to 20 **stories**, but as construction methods have developed, it is now usually used to describe buildings that are far, far taller.

As taller structures are built, new classifications are used:

MEGATALL SKYSCRAPERS
buildings over 2,000 ft

SUPERTALL SKYSCRAPERS
between 1,000 and 2,000 ft

SKYSCRAPERS
between 500 and 1,000 ft

Shanghai World Financial Center

Empire State Building

Eiffel Tower

Great Pyramid of Giza   Tallest   Tallest Redwood tree

WHY BUILD A SKYSCRAPER?

Since ancient times people have built tall structures to show off their wealth and power. Pyramids, cathedrals, and mosques were built to be large and visible. Skyscrapers really took off in New York City in the 1930s, when large companies competed to build the tallest skyscraper in the world.

The practical reason for building upward is to save on ground space. This has become even more important as cities grow and more space is needed to house people and offices.

Skyscrapers in New York City

The Tokyo Sky Tree is the tallest tower in the world, but it has no offices or homes so it's not a skyscraper.

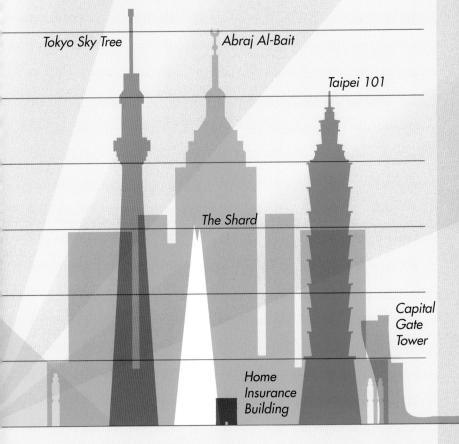

Tokyo Sky Tree

Abraj Al-Bait

Taipei 101

The Shard

Capital Gate Tower

Home Insurance Building

SKYSCRAPER CHALLENGES

Building high brings many challenges. Skyscrapers must be strong enough to support their own weight, plus the **live load,** and sturdy enough to withstand wild weather and even earthquakes.

To ensure a successful and **innovative** skyscraper, teams of **engineers**, **architects**, and **surveyors** need to carefully consider the building brief, plan the design, and choose the correct materials and techniques for the job.

Smart engineering means the sky's the limit for skyscrapers!

HOME INSURANCE BUILDING

Built in Chicago, Illinois, in 1885, the Home Insurance Building is considered to be the first skyscraper in the world. It revolutionized the way buildings were designed and built by introducing strong materials and sparking future ambitions to build higher and higher.

BUILDING BRIEF

Build an office building that makes maximum use of the limited ground space available in Chicago.

Architect: William Le Baron Jenney

Location: Chicago, Illinois, USA

At 180 feet, the Home Insurance Building was not tall by today's standards. It was demolished in 1931 to make way for a taller skyscraper, the Field Building, which is now called the LaSalle Bank Building.

METAL FRAME

The height of the Home Insurance Building was achieved by using a metal frame as a skeleton structure. Architect William Jenney got the idea for building a metal frame after seeing his wife put a large, heavy book on top of a wire birdcage, and it supported the weight of the book easily. Jenney realized that the weight was spread evenly through the thin wires of the cage, making the structure more balanced.

STEEL STRENGTH

At the start of the building process, cast and wrought **iron** were used for the skeleton frame. Partway through, Jenney decided to try a new metal called **steel**. Using steel was such a new idea that worried city officials stopped the construction to check the safety of the building.

Jenney was right to use steel because it is a much better building material than iron. It's lighter, harder, and does not rust as easily. Jenney's innovative engineering changed the way future skyscrapers would be built—with supporting steel frames.

Because a steel frame was supporting the building rather than brick walls, the Home Insurance Building had lots of large windows to light the interior.

Height 180 ft

PYRAMID FOUNDATIONS

Gravity is a constant downward force and as each story is added to a building, the weight increases. To support this weight, there has to be a sturdy base, known as a **foundation**, which is usually built underground. The Home Insurance Building had pyramid-shaped foundations. With the widest area at the bottom and smaller squares on top, this shape helped balance and hold the weight of the building above it. This type of support is called a **spread footing**.

*Several pyramid-shaped foundations were used. They were made from layers of stone, **concrete**, and rubble and were each 20 feet deep.*

7

CHRYSLER BUILDING

In the early 1930s, New York City experienced a building boom with skyscrapers popping up all over town. It was an era of new machinery and technological development, which is reflected in the **iconic** design of the Chrysler Building.

BUILDING BRIEF

Build the tallest and most impressive building in the world. It should work as a **landmark** and an office space for the Chrysler car company.

Architect: William Van Alen

Location: New York City, USA

Height 1,046 ft

RACE FOR THE SKY

Car manufacturer Walter Chrysler wanted a building that was taller and grander than any other in the world. To ensure it was the tallest, the architect added a 125 ft spire that was assembled in secret in the lift shaft. This made the Chrysler Building the tallest building in the world in 1930. But just 11 months later it was overtaken by the Empire State Building, which was built just a few blocks away.

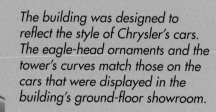

The building was designed to reflect the style of Chrysler's cars. The eagle-head ornaments and the tower's curves match those on the cars that were displayed in the building's ground-floor showroom.

STEEL SKELETON

The Chrysler Building was constructed around a rigid steel frame. **Vertical** steel columns that sit on underground foundations support the weight of the building. **Horizontal** beams attached to the vertical columns support the weight of the roof and each story. The columns and beams were secured using metal pins, called **rivets**.

It's the steel frame, not the surrounding bricks, that hold up the building. The brick covering is called a **curtain wall**. It is attached to the frame and provides decorative weatherproofing but not structural support.

In total, 391,881 rivets were used to bolt the frame of the Chrysler Building together. Rivets are good at supporting **tension loads** because they firmly hold the beams that are trying to pull apart.

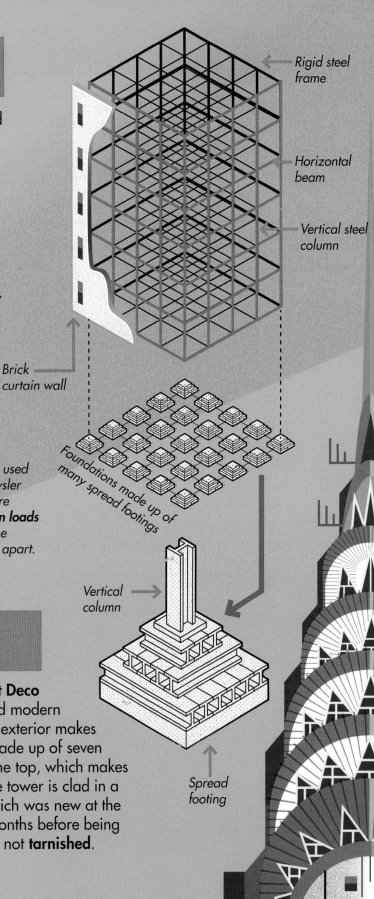

Rigid steel frame

Horizontal beam

Vertical steel column

Brick curtain wall

Tension load

Rivet

Tension load

Foundations made up of many spread footings

Vertical column

Spread footing

EXTERIOR DESIGN

The building is a beautiful example of **Art Deco** design—a popular style that was new and modern in the 1920s and 1930s. The white brick exterior makes it appear light and bright. The tower is made up of seven overlapping arches that narrow toward the top, which makes the building look even taller than it is. The tower is clad in a shimmering steel called Enduro KA-2, which was new at the time. It was tested in rain and wind for months before being used. It has never been replaced and has not **tarnished**.

9

EMPIRE STATE BUILDING

Completed in 1931, the Empire State Building is 1,454 ft tall. It is an iconic landmark of the New York City skyline and is one of the most famous buildings in the world.

BUILDING BRIEF

Build the tallest building in New York City and the world. Design it so that sunlight still reaches the streets below.

Architects:
Shreve, Lamb, and Harmon

Structural engineer:
Homer G. Balcom

Location: New York City, USA

EFFICIENT BUILDING

The design and construction process for the Empire State Building was incredibly efficient. The architectural drawings took only two weeks to be completed, and the building process ran on a strict schedule with a construction rate of four-and-a-half stories completed each week.

It was built at a time of change in the building industry. New ways of working were introduced, such as assembly lines, delivering pieces on specially laid rail tracks, and having chutes that allowed the bricks to be dropped and hoisted around the site. This made things speedy, reduced the use of workers pushing wheelbarrows, and kept the surrounding area clear of building materials.

Height 1,454 ft

ELEVATORS

The rise of skyscrapers would not have been possible without the invention of the safety elevator in 1853. Nobody wants to live or work in a 100-story building where stairs are the only way to get to the top! A steel support frame surrounds the elevators located in the center of the Empire State Building. This adds further stability to the skyscraper's inner core.

A worker with no fear of heights fixes a beam in place.

When it opened, the Empire State Building had 64 elevators. Today it has 73.

Steel supports around the elevators

Original floor plan of the 58th floor

HEIGHT

As more skyscrapers were built, New York City introduced a law requiring tall buildings to **taper** as they go up to allow sunlight to reach the city streets below. This can be seen in the Empire State Building's design. It decreases in size as it rises to the **apex**. The staggered shape of the building also has a structural advantage, as the larger sections below support the smaller sections above.

The Empire State Building has been seen in nearly 200 films. Its most famous appearance was in King Kong (1933 and 2005), when it was climbed by the giant gorilla.

Tapered apex

The mast at the top of the Empire State Building was designed as a place to tether airships. In practice this proved too dangerous because strong winds swirling up the sides of the building caused the airships to blow around, making them highly unstable.

11

WILLIS TOWER

Originally known as the Sears Tower, the Willis Tower was completed in 1973 using a new way of grouping steel frames together. This revolutionized skyscraper design and allowed buildings to be taller, stronger, cheaper, as well as more architecturally interesting.

BUILDING BRIEF

Use a new and innovative design to construct an office building to house the headquarters of the biggest retailer in the world.

Architect: Bruce Graham at Skidmore, Owings, and Merrill

Structural engineer: Fazlur Rahman Khan

Location: Chicago, Illinois, USA

BUNDLED TUBE STRUCTURE

Structural engineer Fazlur Khan came up with a new way to construct skyscrapers using a bundled tube structure system. This places multiple steel frames alongside each other. Clustered together, they provide greater strength and resistance to wind, earthquakes, and **stress** from the upper weight of the building. The Willis Tower uses a bundle of nine steel frames.

"When thinking design, I put myself in the place of a whole building, feeling every part. In my mind I visualize the stresses and twisting a building undergoes."

Fazlur Khan, Engineer

Bundled tube structure and floor plan

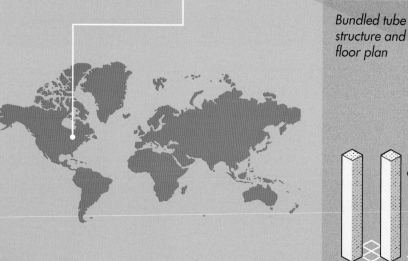

Placing smaller frames around the outside supports the weight of the tallest frames

CANTILEVER

The bundled tube structure uses the smaller tube frames around the outside to act as a support for the taller frames. They resist the sideway and downward loads of the taller frames and distribute the weight through the building. This is called a **cantilever** when a section can successfully extend outward or upward because it is well supported by the main structure. It's like a giant diving board that's held in place at one end.

Stories 91–108

Stories 67–90

Stories 51–66

Stories 1–50

Skydeck

Height 1,729 ft

Tallest building in the world from 1973 to 1998

SKYDECK

The Skydeck was added to the tower in 1974. It was made from retractable glass boxes, 1,353 ft above the ground. They are held in place on steel cantilevers that are fixed into the side of the building. The boxes can move out from the face of the building on rails.

←4.3 ft→

The boxes are supported on steel cantilever rails hidden inside the building.

Each Skydeck box is made from three layers of half-inch thick glass with a strong thin steel frame at the edge. It gives occupants the impression of being suspended in air.

PETRONAS TWIN TOWERS

At 1,483 ft high, the Petronas Twin Towers are the tallest twin-tower skyscrapers in the world. They were designed to be the focus of the skyline in Kuala Lumpur, the capital city of Malaysia. Engineers had to contend with the soft soil and strong winds during the planning and construction.

BUILDING BRIEF

Build a twin-towered skyscraper to house businesses and shops. It should reflect the **culture** of Malaysia and Islamic architectural style. It must be able to withstand wind speeds of 65 miles per hour (mph).

Architect: César Pelli

Structural engineer: Thornton Tomasetti

Location: Kuala Lumpur, Malaysia

MOVING BRIDGE

The two towers are connected on the 41st and 42nd floors by the Skybridge. The Skybridge was constructed so that it was not fixed to either tower but can slide in and out. High winds cause the towers to sway and move away from each other by up to 30 inches. If the Skybridge was fixed in place, winds would easily damage it.

The Skybridge is supported underneath by a triangular arch. This flexes on **spherical** bearings, which allow movement and work in a similar way to the human hip joint.

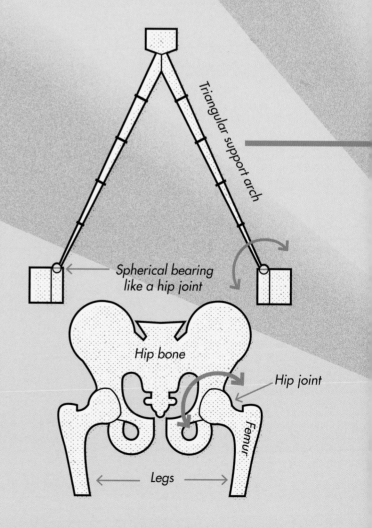

Triangular support arch

Spherical bearing like a hip joint

Hip bone

Hip joint

Femur

Legs

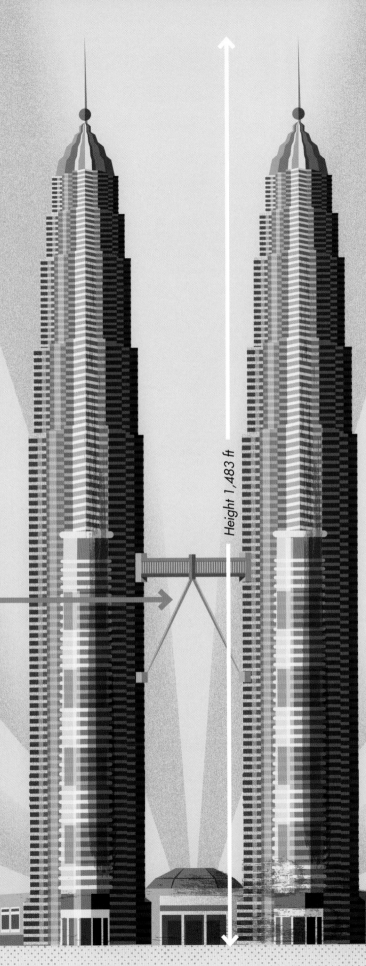

Height 1,483 ft

FOUNDATIONS

Early in development, it was discovered that the ground was too soft to support the towers' weight. So the engineers and designers had to build really deep foundations, digging down until they hit strong **limestone** rock. They filled the space between the surface and the limestone with 104 concrete piles of varying lengths for each tower. The shortest pile was about 200 ft in length and the longest was 375 ft.

CONCRETE

The towers were built using concrete with steel rods running through it, which is known as reinforced concrete. This was cheaper than using a steel frame because less steel needed to be imported. Reinforced concrete is more rigid, so it is better at reducing a building's sway. However, it does make the finished building much heavier. But that's not much of a problem when you have the world's deepest foundation.

Steel rods →

Concrete →

Reinforced concrete

30 ST. MARY AXE

The skyline of London is filled with many unusually shaped skyscrapers, including 30 St. Mary Axe. Also known as the Gherkin due to its cylindrical shape, its eye-catching design fulfills the practical needs of the space both inside and outside the building.

BUILDING BRIEF

Build an energy-saving office building in the financial district of London. It needs to fit within the exact space of the previous building on that site and have a new and exciting design.

Architects: Norman Foster and Ken Shuttleworth

Structural engineer: Arup

Location: London, England

Height 590 ft

A DIAGRID

30 St. Mary Axe has a supporting steel framework called a diagrid. This means that the framework is made from diagonally intersecting ribs of steel that are welded or bolted together.

To support the weight of the building, the diagrid distributes loads in a downward zigzag pattern through the diagonal beams. This removes the need for vertical columns inside, which allows for more space and light throughout the building.

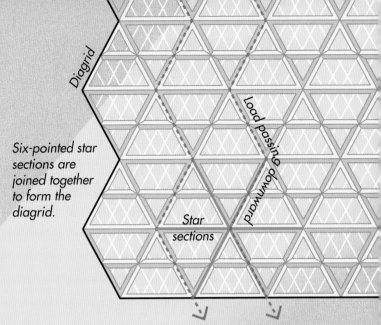

Six-pointed star sections are joined together to form the diagrid.

The diagrid can be seen in the diamond and triangular patterns on the building's exterior.

"[Diagrid is] a series of triangles that combine gravity and lateral support into one, making the building stiff, efficient, and lighter than a traditional high-rise."

Yoram Eilon, Project Manager for Cantor Seinuk

ENERGY EFFICIENT

The weather and the use of computers have created a heating system that uses half the energy of other skyscrapers this size. Air blowing against the exterior of the building is allowed in through gaps in the walls. Once inside, the air is warmed through the external glass. This process is called solar gain. A computer system constantly monitors the temperature of the building and opens the windows when it gets too hot.

COMPUTER DESIGN

Early plans for the building were tested using a modeling software usually used in the design of airplanes and spacecraft. The tests revealed that flat panes of glass could be used rather than pieces of curved glass. In fact, curved glass is only used right at the top of the building.

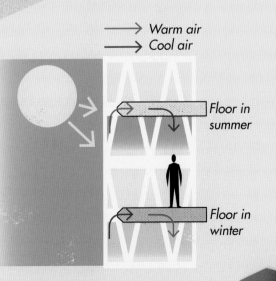

Warm air
Cool air

Floor in summer

Floor in winter

TAIPEI 101

At 1,667 ft, Taipei 101 is one of the tallest skyscrapers in the world. It stands in Taiwan's capital city, Taipei, less than 1/8 mile from a major **fault line**—an area of earthquake activity.

BUILDING BRIEF

Build a landmark iconic skyscraper that can withstand typhoon winds and earthquakes.

Architects: C. Y. Lee & Partners

Structural engineer: Thornton Tomasetti

Location: Taipei, Taiwan

GIANT PENDULUM

Taipei 101 has an unusual engineering feature that hangs between its 88th and 92nd floors: a large steel sphere, called a tuned mass damper (TMD). This acts as a giant **pendulum** that moves slightly back and forth to reduce any movement of the building.

When an earthquake strikes, the TMD swings in the same direction as the sway of the building but with a time lag. This reduces the amount of sway.

The foundations are sunk more than 250 ft into the ground.

In 1999, an earthquake in Taipei destroyed more than 10,000 buildings.

Taipei 101 is named after its home city and the number of floors it has above ground—101.

Taipei 101's TMD is the largest in the world. It is 18 ft in diameter and weighs 730 tons.

Height 1,667 ft

MEGA-COLUMNS

Taipei 101's exterior has eight mega-columns. These are steel columns packed with super-strong concrete. The mega-columns are connected to each other with **belt trusses**. **Outriggers**—beams that reach across a structure to help stabilize its frame—connect the mega-columns to internal steel columns.

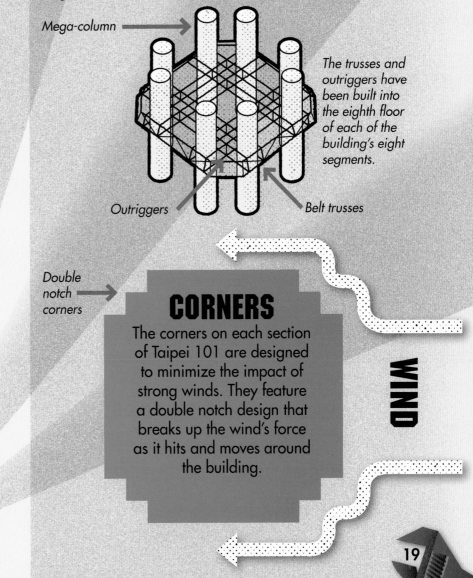

Mega-column

The trusses and outriggers have been built into the eighth floor of each of the building's eight segments.

Outriggers

Belt trusses

Double notch corners

CORNERS

The corners on each section of Taipei 101 are designed to minimize the impact of strong winds. They feature a double notch design that breaks up the wind's force as it hits and moves around the building.

WIND

BAHRAIN WORLD TRADE CENTER

Built in 2008, the Bahrain World Trade Center is the world's first wind-powered skyscraper. The 787 foot-tall twin towers are linked by three bridges, each supporting a giant wind **turbine**.

BUILDING BRIEF

Build a new trade center to add a focal point to a revitalized part of the city of Manama. Give some thought to the sustainability and eco-friendliness of the building.

Architect: Shaun Killa at Atkins

Structural engineer: Atkins

Location: Manama, Bahrain

This view of the Manama skyline shows the towering Bahrain World Trade Center.

AIRFOIL SAILS

Situated right next to the Persian Gulf, the building looks like an enormous sailboat. However the design is more than just decorative. The shape of the towers helps to power the wind turbines that sit between them.

From overhead, each tower appears **elliptical**, like the airfoil shape of an airplane wing. This shape helps funnel air from the gulf straight toward the turbines between the two curved towers.

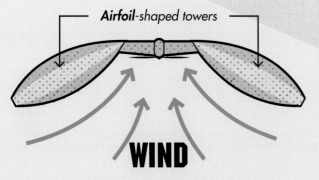

Airfoil-shaped towers

WIND

Overhead view of Bahrain World Trade Center

WIND POWER

Buildings consume a third of the world's energy, so it's important that they become more energy-efficient. Architect Shaun Killa designed the Bahrain WTC to have a self-generating power source—wind turbines. Each turbine is 95 ft in diameter, and as they turn, they produce 11–15 percent of the power needed for the entire building.

Height 787 ft

HOW THEY WORK

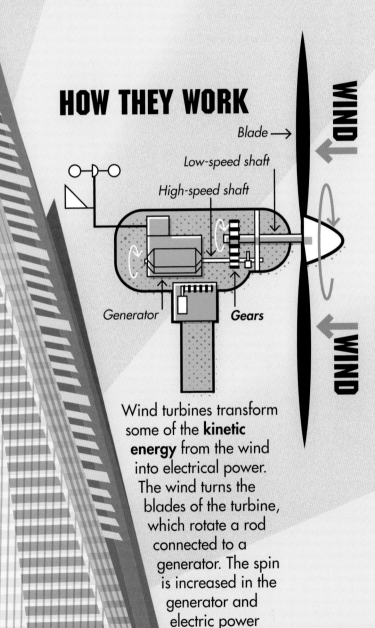

Blade →

Low-speed shaft

High-speed shaft

Generator

Gears

WIND

WIND

Wind turbines transform some of the **kinetic energy** from the wind into electrical power. The wind turns the blades of the turbine, which rotate a rod connected to a generator. The spin is increased in the generator and electric power is produced.

BURJ KHALIFA

In 2009, Burj Khalifa became the tallest building in the world. At 2,723 ft high, it belongs to a growing number of megatall skyscrapers. It's an impressive landmark and a hard-to-miss sight in Dubai, one of the planet's fastest-growing cities.

BUILDING BRIEF

Build a centerpiece for downtown Dubai, an expanding area of homes and hotels. Make it impressive enough to attract visitors and businesses to the country.

Architect: Adrian Smith at Skidmore, Owings, and Merrill

Structural engineer: Bill Baker

Location: Dubai, UAE

Height 2,723 ft

BUTTRESSED CORE

Burj Khalifa uses a bundled tube structure (see page 12), and has a hexagonal frame, called the buttressed core, at the center of the building. This acts like a mega-strong spine supporting the building as it rises. The buttressed core is supported at ground level by three outward sections.

As the building rises, the tower tapers in 27 different places to form an ascending spiral, a complex but sturdy design. The buttressed core emerges from the top of the building like a giant **minaret** tower on a mosque.

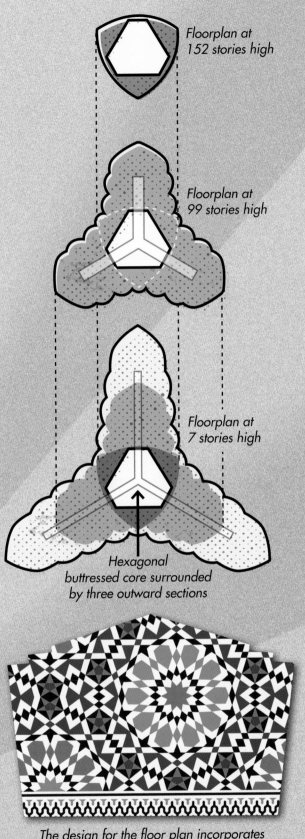

Floorplan at 152 stories high

Floorplan at 99 stories high

Floorplan at 7 stories high

Hexagonal buttressed core surrounded by three outward sections

The design for the floor plan incorporates traditional pentagon and triangle patterns, which are typical of the Islamic style.

CONFUSING THE WIND

With its tapering and jagged sides, the design of the Burj Khalifa reduces the strength of the wind. When wind hits the exterior of the building, it is deflected at different speeds and directions, which reduces its power to damage the building. The exterior design went through 40 different tests in wind tunnels to ensure it would stand up well to strong winds.

This diagram shows how the design of the building at different heights deflects the wind in various ways.

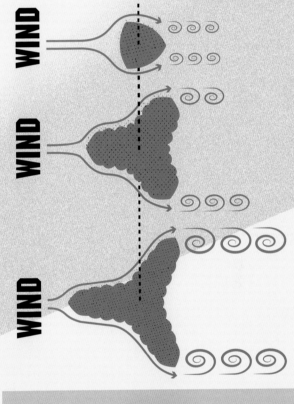

SWAY

Burj Khalifa can sway 5 ft at the top. This may sound dramatic, but the structure has to give a little with the wind. If it was engineered to be totally rigid and didn't move, it would put too much stress on the whole building and risk it falling over. Like branches on a tree, buildings have to sway a bit.

BOSCO VERTICALE

Italian for "vertical forest," Bosco Verticale is the name of a pair of eco-friendly buildings built in Milan, Italy, in 2014. They may not be supertall skyscrapers, but they are super-innovative, merging structural and landscape design so that high-rise living doesn't mean living without a garden.

BUILDING BRIEF

Build a residential block for the busy city of Milan. It should promote sustainability and biodiversity and reduce air, heat, and noise pollution for the residents.

Architects: Stefano Boeri, Gianandrea Barreca, Giovanni La Varra at Boeri Studio

Location: Milan, Italy

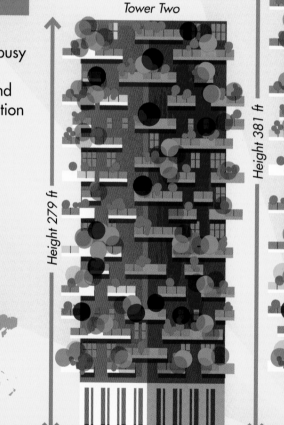

Tower One

Tower Two

Height 279 ft

Height 381 ft

URBAN FOREST

Architect Stefano Boeri wanted the Bosco Verticale to have a living facade that would change and grow over the seasons. He talked with **botanists** for two years to plan which plants would thrive above the city, coming up with over 90 different species. The balconies on the 26 floors of Tower One and 18 floors of Tower Two are home to more than 730 trees, 5,000 shrubs, and 11,000 **perennial plants**!

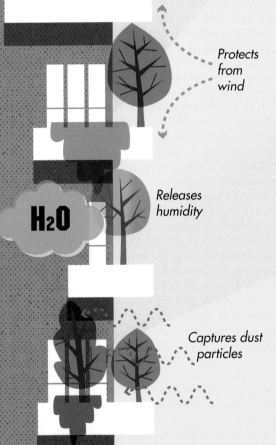

Provides shade

Lets in light during the winter

Protects from wind

H₂O

Releases humidity

Captures dust particles

O₂ **CO₂** Produces oxygen

Reduces noise pollution

BIOCLIMATIC

The towers were built to be "bioclimatic." Bioclimatic architecture connects directly with nature, taking into account the climate and environmental conditions of its location. The green screen planting on the Bosco Veticale helps to cut down on air pollution by absorbing **carbon monoxide**. It also reduces noise from the busy streets, filters dust, and helps regulate the temperature inside, keeping it warmer in winter and cooler in summer.

The design provides a lovely garden view for the occupants and helps soften the hard edges of the exterior.

HEAVY SUPPORT

Reinforced concrete beams are used throughout the buildings, which makes them very heavy but also very strong. This is essential for supporting the weight of the plants that live there and the soil they need. The balconies have a cantilever design with the supported end secured inside the building. They extend 11 ft outward with trees planted on the edge and tied into place so that they don't fall and damage the building or the street below.

SHANGHAI TOWER

At 2,073 ft, the Shanghai Tower is one of the tallest buildings in the world. Completed in 2015, its twisting cutting-edge design helps make it one of the most sustainable mega-tall towers and a landmark design for future skyscrapers.

The Shanghai Tower (right) completes a trio of skyscrapers in the city's financial district. It stands alongside the Jin Mao Tower (center) and the Shanghai World Financial Center (left).

BUILDING BRIEF

Design an eco-friendly building to provide lots of office space, plus community areas for people to enjoy.

Architects: Daniel Winey, Jun Xia, and Marshall Strabala at Gensler

Structural engineers: Thornton Tomasetti

Location: Shanghai, China

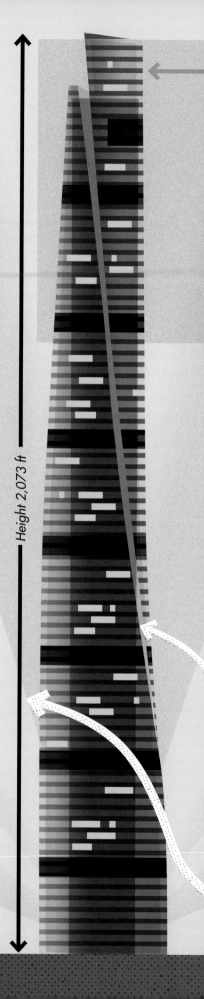

Height 2,073 ft

GREEN POWER

The Shanghai Tower claims to be the greenest skyscraper in the world. Its energy needs are supplied from different sources, including wind turbines, solar panels, and **geothermal energy**. There are 200 wind turbines located 1,900 ft up, near the top of the building. The wind speed is fast up there, driving the turbines to produce about 10 percent of the building's electricity.

WIND

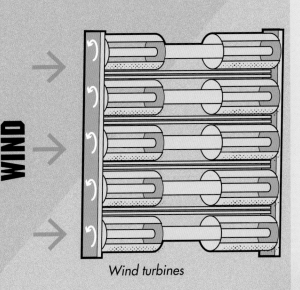

Wind turbines

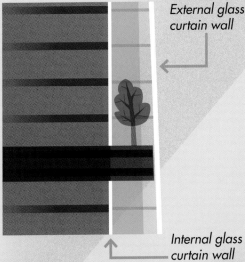

External glass curtain wall

Internal glass curtain wall

There are nine areas between the glass walls that contain public spaces and sky gardens.

GLASS

The Shanghai Tower was built with two glass curtain walls that help control the internal temperature of the building. The space between the glass warms the cool air in winter and reduces the heat in summer, making it very energy efficient.

Most skyscrapers use tinted, reflective glass that's designed to lower the absorption of heat. The success of the Shanghai Tower's double glass layer design meant that it could be built with transparent glass. This allows people to see in and out of the building and lets more light inside.

TWISTING SHAPE

The facade's unique twisting shape turns and tapers toward the top. This design reduces the amount of wind hitting the tower by 24 percent, and it can even withstand typhoons.

"[This building] is about China's future, which is more transparent, more open — it's a building for people."

Marshall Strabala, Architect

FASCINATING FACTS

Skyscrapers come in many weird and wonderful forms. Here is a collection of awesome skyscraper facts from all around the world.

No city in the world has more skyscrapers than Hong Kong. The highest of all is the International Commerce Center, which was completed in 2010 and is 1,588 ft tall.

It's all very well building massively tall glass skyscrapers, but how in the world do you clean the windows? Each of the Petronas Twin Towers has around 16,000 panes of glass. Window-washing platforms extend out of hidden compartments at the top of the buildings. It takes two months to clean both towers!

At 1,004 ft tall, the Shard in London is one of Europe's tallest buildings. The building got its name because the exterior looks like shards of glass balanced against each other. The shimmering exterior is made up of 11,000 glass panels, and an amazing 95 percent of the materials used to build it were recycled.

Home Insurance Building   The Elephant Tower   Bosco Verticale   Guangzhou Circle   30 St. Mary Axe   The Turning Torso   Bahrain World Trade Center   The Shard

STRANGE SHAPES

The Turning Torso in Malmo, Sweden, is the tallest building in Scandinavia. The inspiration for the twisting building is a turning human body.

The tallest circular skyscraper in the world is the Guangzhou Circle in China. It's 452 ft tall and was built in 2014. The building's design is based on important Chinese symbols.

Built in 1997, the Elephant Tower in Bangkok looks like its name implies: it's a building in the shape of an elephant, Thailand's national animal. The elephant's ears are giant balconies and its eyes are windows.

Height in feet

2,970	
2,640	
2,310	
1,980	
1,650	
1,320	
990	
660	
330	
0	

Chrysler Building | Empire State Building | Petronas Twin Towers | International Commerce Center | Taipei 101 | Willis Tower | Shanghai Tower | Burj Khalifa

READ MORE

Burns, Kylie. *A Skyscraper Reaches Up.* Be an Engineer! Designing to Solve Problems. New York: Crabtree Publishing Company, 2017.

Duke, Shirley. *Skyscrapers and Towers.* Engineering Wonders. Vero Beach, Fla.: Rourke Educational Media, 2015.

Finger, Brad. *13 Skyscrapers Children Should Know.* Children Should Know. New York: Prestel Publishing, 2016.

Ventura, Marne. *Building Skyscrapers.* Engineering Challenges. Mendota Heights, Minn.: North Star Editions, 2017.

INTERNET SITES

FactHound offers a safe, fun way to find Internet sites related to this book. All of the sites on FactHound have been researched by our staff.

Here's all you do:

Visit www.facthound.com

Type in this code: 9781543513332

Super-cool stuff! Check out projects, games and lots more at
www.capstonekids.com

GLOSSARY

airfoil an airplane surface, such as a wing or rudder, designed to produce a reaction from the air through which it moves; air flows faster over the top of an airfoil shape and slower underneath it

apex the uppermost point of something

architect a person who designs and often supervises the construction of buildings

Art Deco a design style of the 1920s and 1930s, using geometric shapes and bold colors

belt truss a framework usually consisting of rafters, posts, and struts that tie together and support a roof, bridge, or other structure

botanist a scientist who studies plants

cantilever a beam fastened at only one end

carbon monoxide a poisonous gas produced by the engines of vehicles

concrete a building material made from a mixture of sand, gravel, cement, and water

culture a group of people's beliefs, customs, and way of life

curtain wall an exterior wall that does not support the roof or the building

elliptical shaped like an oval

engineer someone who designs and builds roads, machines, vehicles, bridges, or other structures

fault line a crack in the earth where two plates meet; earthquakes often occur along fault lines

foundation a solid structure on which a building is built

gear a toothed wheel that fits into another toothed wheel; gears can change the direction of a force or can transfer power

geothermal energy energy that comes from the intense heat inside the earth.

gravity a force that pulls objects with mass together; gravity pulls objects down toward the center of Earth

horizontal flat and parallel to the ground

iconic an object or person that is famous, popular, and admired

innovative advanced or unlike anything done before

iron a hard metal used in buildings; cast iron is made from an alloy of iron, carbon, and silicon

kinetic energy the energy of a moving object

landmark an object that stands out as important, such as a big tree or a building

limestone a hard white or gray stone, often used as a building material

live load the total force or weight that a structure is designed to withstand or hold

minaret a tall slender tower of a mosque with a balcony

outrigger a beam that projects beyond a wall to support an overhanging roof or extended floor.

pendulum a weight that swings back and forth from a fixed point

perennial plant a plant that lives for more than two years

rivet a metal bolt or pin used to hold metal objects together

spherical having a solid round form like that of a basketball or globe

spread footing a footing in building construction that is shallow in proportion to its width and is usually made of reinforced concrete

steel a strong, hard metal formed from iron, carbon, and other materials

story a level of a building

stress the physical pressure, pull, or other force on an object

surveyor someone who measures areas of land for builders or mapmakers

taper to become progressively smaller toward one end

tarnish to make or become dull, dim, or discolored

tension load a pulling force

turbine a machine with blades that can be turned by wind or a moving fluid, such as steam or water, to produce electricity

vertical straight up and down

INDEX